Chloe flaherty ♡

happy birthday

summersdale

To: Chloe Flaherty

From: Mummy daddy
Emma and aaron
Hollie

Summersdale Publishers Ltd
46 West Street
Chichester
West Sussex
PO19 1RP
UK

www.summersdale.com

Printed and bound by Tien Wah Press, Singapore

ISBN: 978-1-84024-763-3

Substantial discounts on bulk quantities of Summersdale books are available to corporations, professional associations and other organisations. For details telephone Summersdale Publishers on (+44-1243-771107), fax (+44-1243-786300) or email (nicky@summersdale.com).

happy birthday

Poppy Bell

It's your special day!

So wake up with
a big smile...

... or enjoy a lazy morning in bed...

… then put on your party outfit.

Come rain or shine…

... today you can feel bright and breezy.

Everyone will be
thinking of you.

Remember that good things come in small packages...

... and the best gift of all is love.

No present is as precious
or beautiful as you.

It's time to indulge in all
your favourite treats.

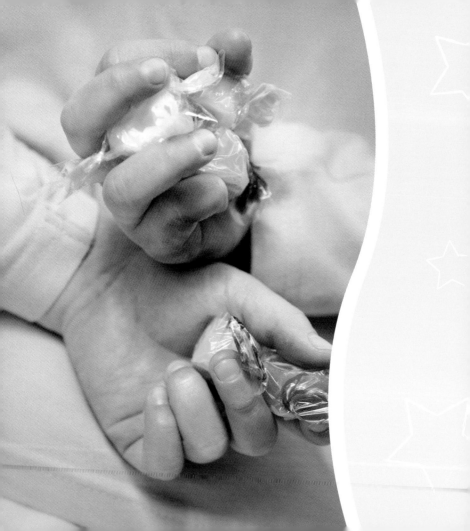

You don't even
have to share...

... but don't get
too carried away!

Birthdays are for fun...

... maybe you'll have a
picnic in the park...

... spend a day
in the great
outdoors...

… lounge around
at home…

… or catch up with an old friend.

Take a moment to appreciate life's simple pleasures…

... and save enough breath
to blow out those candles.

It's time to celebrate!

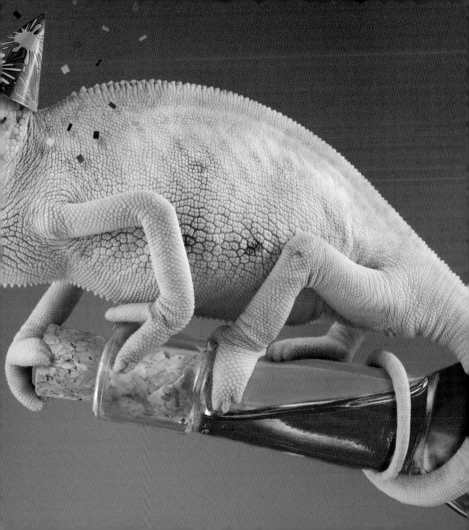

You're going to be the centre of attention…

... because you're
a star...

... and a real sweetie.

You're great
company…

... if a little silly
at times.

There's no one else
quite like you…

Maybe someone's planning
a surprise for you.

You can rely on your true
friends to celebrate with you.

So get into the
party spirit...

… and show off
those moves!

Hold on to those balloons!

Yes, birthdays can be
quite exhausting…

... but from when
you're a child...

... to when you're grumpy and old...

… birthdays hold
special memories.

Remember: you're only
as old as your heart...

... and birthdays are good for you.
The more you have, the better.

Don't be sad when it's over...

... there'll be many
more happy occasions.

So here's a
birthday kiss…

... and a toast to you!

Happy birthday!

Have you enjoyed this book? If so, why not write a review on your favourite website?

Thanks very much for buying this Summersdale book.

www.summersdale.com

Chloe
Flaherty